Snapshots through Time

Poems about Struggling, Healing, Growth and Enlightenment

NELLA COIRO

Snapshots through Time

Copyright © 2024 by Nella Coiro

ISBN: Print: 978-1-7339522-5-5
E-book: 978-1-7339522-6-2
Library of Congress Control Number: 2023911540

Published in the United States by
Sunrise Valley Publishers

"Our tears become holy in the form of ink on a page. Once we have spoken our saddest story, we can be free of it. And then all that's left behind is the tortured poetry."

Taylor Swift

CONTENTS

Prologue 1
Chapter 1 – Childhood (Death from a Thousand Cuts) 2
    Death from a Thousand Cuts 3
    The Dark Years (A Little Girl's Tears) 4
    The Dinner Hour 5
    Junior Mints 6
    The Dry Well 7
    Swept Away 8
    Tie-Dye & Love Beads 10
    The Terrified Rebel 11
    Memories of My Father 12
    Barbie Dolls & Other Losses 13
    Dusty Remnants 14
    Then and Now, in Four Chapters 15
Chapter 2 – Mothers 18
    Old Photos 19
    The Serrated Steak Knife 20
    The Toxic Dance 21
    The Night My Mother Died 22
    The Wake 23
    The Voice 25
    Tumbling Down 27
    One Hundred Pennies (The Will) 28
Chapter 3 – Adopted 30
    Adopted 31
    The Screaming Truth 33
    Origins 34
    Dear Birth Mom 35
Chapter 4 – Sisters 36

a Free And New Non-toxIc lifE 37
The Ice Queen (Fannieng Toxicity) 38
Earnestly Earned Karma 39
Guitars & Lipstick 40
The Competition 41
Unreciprocated Love 43
My Sister's Her-i-cane 44
Her Mother's Daughter 45
The Turbulent Winds 46
Getting Wet 47
Exiting Hell 48
Banished 50
Fading to Invisible 51

Chapter 5 - Scraps of Sadness 54
Scraps of Sadness 55
Carousels 56
Frozen in Time 57
Bursts of Darkness 58
Lost in Sadness 60
Grief is a Sentient Being 61
Colors of Sadness 63

Chapter 6 – Pensive Ponderings 64
Diamonds 65
Letting Go 66
Less Lost 68
Lucky Alex 69
Touching an Emotion 70
The Clock 71
Dreams and Lint 73
Dingy Memories 74
Loose Ends 76

The Stylus..77
Chapter 7 – The Dialysis Journey..............................78
  A Bucket of Ice Water...79
  The Dialysis Path..81
  The Dialysis Machine...84
  Dialysis, A Day at a Time...85
  Dialysis Reflections, Tongue-in-Cheek.....................87
Chapter 8 – Spirituality...90
  God's Presence...91
  Spiritual Simplicity...93
  Miracles...94
  Been There...96
  Finding God in the Darkness......................................97
  The Shroud (A Simple Prayer)....................................98
  A Silent Whisper...99
Chapter 9 – Random Reflections...............................100
  Peter Pan...101
  Forgiveness Revisited...102
  Melting Snowflakes..103
  Goodbyes..104
  Windswept...105
  Just Tales..107
  Dream-mares...109
  Uneven Exchanges...110
  Unsteadiness...111
  Carousel of Absurdity..112
  The Sidewalk...113
  Gashes & Slashes...114
  The Measure of a Life..115
  Battle Wounds...116
  It Was Alcohol..117

A Patient Boomerang 119
Insomnia 120
The Middle 121
Snapshots through Time 122
Chapter 10 – Growth, Healing & Enlightenment 124
The Meat Grinder 125
The Darts and the Dart Board 126
Glinda's Words 127
Bubbling Hot Coffee (Trauma Drama) 128
Recovery 130
Soul Mate Reflections 131
Changes 132
Dancing in the Rain 133
Evolving and Becoming 135
Animal Companions 136
Purple Hearts 137
My Inner Knight 138
Paying Attention 140
Forward Bound 141
Sticks & Stones 142
Still Standing 143
Moments Etched in Time 144
The Phoenix 145
Intoxicating Toxicity 146
Transfusion and Rebirth 147
Long Story Short 148
My Life Manuscript 149
What is Hope? 150
What if? 151
Epilogue 153
A Message from the Author 155

Other Titles by this Author 155
Acknowledgements 156
In Loving Memory 156

Prologue

I don't remember shedding many tears when I was growing up. And yet, at the same time, my heart was hemorrhaging sorrow and pain. I think that my sadness morphed into words on a page. My tears dripped onto the blank looseleaf sheet, became a poem or a song, and then evaporated, appeared to disappear, and temporarily provided some relief and healing. But the thing is, they really didn't disappear completely. Instead, they just hid inside a closet, and effected my life in covert, yet powerful ways.

Throughout my life, and up to the present time, writing has been the primary way in which I've been able to document my journey, and to vent and give expression to my feelings, experiences, struggles, insights, healing, growth, and, what I consider to be enlightenment.

I've written this book of poetry for several different readers: those who seek hope and inspiration; those who need the comfort of knowing that they're not alone; and to all those who have experienced adversities in life, but have absolutely refused to give up! Instead, they have chosen to use their experiences to learn, to heal, to grow, and to help others. Every sentiment and emotion encapsulated in every poem in this book has an important tale to tell. They are my *snapshots through time.*

Chapter 1 – Childhood
(Death from a Thousand Cuts)

Death from a Thousand Cuts

My childhood was a grueling, gradual death
From a thousand cuts and slices.
Stealing my lungs of life sustaining breath...
Attempts to dim my spiritual brightness.

Tossed fears & threats at me
Like chunks of red-hot coal.
Intimidation & submission.
This was their goal.

But...
Ultimately...
They failed
To break me...

The Dark Years... A Little Girl's Tears

There was a time, perhaps age three or five,
When I felt joy was a possibility in my life.
Dreams of happily dancing in floral gardens,
Until reality coldly severed it like a knife.

Then the flowers lost their joyful brilliance,
And looked terribly frightened and sad.
And dark clouds took charge of the sky,
And fiercely bid the sun "goodbye."

Santa Claus and the Easter Bunny died.
They were brutally murdered!
So I was left all alone
To handle things on my own.

I once thought life could be like the land of Oz.
Perhaps when I was still yet in the crib.
And then life became a cold and hellish web,
With anguish, violence, and no way to get out.

But there was a time
Before all of this little girl's tears,
When I felt joy was
A real possibility in my life...

And now the past does not have to exist,
If I could only extinguish it from my mind!
And perhaps this will be the only way to find
The joy I've longed for before all of those dark years.

The Dinner Hour

Dinner time, the worst time of the day,
Seated both in silence and dismay.
As mom cracks the whip on her command,
We all crumble, afraid to take a stand.

She engages in her usual berating,
While deep within, I felt my anguish grating.
My stomach churns, my appetite is gone,
As her caustic words drone on and on and on...

Her cigarette ashes seasoning the food,
And my stomach burns with every bite I chew.
Forced to leave all of my thoughts unspoken,
While it feels like I'm chewing glass that's broken...

I feel trapped at the table, terrified with fears.
Trying to hold back a massive flood of tears.
Her intimidating icy presence, suffocating.
Attacking us all with endless deprecating.

Recalling the memories
Of a frightened, helpless child.
When every moment, and meal was
An endless walk through hell.

And the frightening sorcerer –
My Mother, who daily cast her spell...

Junior Mints

In my childhood home,
My mom consumed
Mega doses of Valium
With Cavalier Casualness,

Akin to tasting
Tidbits of tasty treats,
Or snacking on
Junior Mints.

Nearly every situation
Triggered anxiety,
Or... an excuse
Which induced
The benzo abuse...

And required:
The tranquil magic...
The expectation
Of the soothing sedation.

The warm cuddly
Comforting feeling
Of a Valium...

My mom's version of
A Junior mint.

The Dry Well

I have tried to love those
With hearts contaminated.
Unsuccessfully, since their
Noxious darkness dominated.

I wanted what
Simply did not exist.
Yet, blinded by a deceiving
Deceiving, alluring abyss...

Shouting down the dry well,
"Give me water, please!"
Weeping, gasping,
And falling to my knees.

And my heart,
Profusely bleeding,
Since the dry well
Always left me needing...

Swept Away

I would cling to the passing wind,
Hoping to be swept away.
But no magic potions did I find
That could soothe my dismay.
They were Swept, Swept,
Swept Away...

Immersed in the quicksand of hopelessness,
The deep darkness obscured my path,
And the frightening thought
Of Another Day, and Another Day...
And Another Day...

Dreams of heroic rescues, and being saved,
But Don Quixote was busy fighting windmills,
Superman quickly flew in the opposite direction,
And Batman timidity hid in his bat cave.

Frightened, weary, and no longer brave.
I hopelessly gave up,
Feeling Saddened and Stranded...
By Hope Abandoned...

Shouting whispered pleas
To those who looked the other way.
Appeals just echoed and blew away
Like beige beach sand on a windy day.
Going... Going... Gone...

Teary-eyed and sadly waving goodbye
To hopes that melted in the sun...
One by One... One by One...
Until One became None...

Hope was swept to the curb,
And washed away by the rain
Again... And Again...
And Again...

Tie-Dye & Love Beads

As a teenager,
I identified with the hippie:

I felt like an outcast...
Damaged.
Diminished.
Different.

Out of synch
With the world.
My heart,
It felt soiled.

An angry rebel.
A rebellious loner.
A Frightened
Forlorn
Lonely loner...

No drugs, no weed,
Or pills of any kind.
But some fond memories of
Boone's Farm Strawberry Hill Wine.
I was a hippie wannabe.
Darned in tie-dye, love beads,
And a fantasy
Of escaping the chaotic reality –
I was trapped in.

The Terrified Rebel

I was called the rebel child,
Yet I bravely stood my ground,
Too young to comprehend
This path was peril bound.

In times of cold foreboding
It was hope that kept me going.
With dreams of better days.
And faith that I'd find ways
To exit from this maze.

Alas...
The thundering,
Deafening silence
That fuels family
Hidden violence...

Memories of My Father

I barely remember my father...
Just blurry bits and pieces,
Like old, weathered snapshots,
Faded, with lines and creases.

I do recall his smile,
Or that he called me "doll."
Often tearful and forlorn,
As if life rendered him battle worn.

He had a blue iridescent suit.
His – Only – Suit.
He wore it to weddings & funerals.
Now... sadly... his own funeral.

His Wake was
Standing room only.
Hundreds of people
"Paying their respects."

Tears – Stories – Endearing comments:

He was a good man. Too young to die.
Whenever you needed help, he was always there.
He fixed my sink. I offered to pay him,
and he said, "Don't insult me. I don't want any money.
But I'll take a cup of coffee." Then he laughed.

My father was a complicated man.
He was many things to many people.
Very few knew his unhappy, dark, troubled side.
Most just knew the helpful, lovable, upbeat guy.

Barbie Dolls & Other Losses

I remember
Our Barbie dolls,
Irreverently tossed away,
Without compassion, or
An iota of dismay.

Our Barbie dolls...
Cherished, Cared for,
Nurtured, Enjoyed.
Poof! Gone in a heartbeat.

Chunks of our world
Casually cast away
Without our consent.
Ignoring our dissent.

Symbolic of so many other losses:
Our father. Our home.
Our friends. Our neighborhood.
Our many possessions.
Cherished priceless pieces
Of our personal history.

Too – many – losses
Piling on top of one another,
Like a unexpected car accident
With multiple casualties.

Dusty Remnants

My parents were complicated,
With overlapping,
Knotty and thorny layers
And old dusty remnants

Of their own
Troubled,
Traumatic,
Unacknowledged
Unhealed
Childhoods.

And, tragically,
Since denied,
Unaddressed,
And hidden away
In a dingy dark closet,

They bequeathed
Some of these
Dusty remnants
Onto their children.

Then and Now, in Four Chapters

-1-

"The deep colors of loneliness grasp me.
I am trapped in a trance,
Suspended within time and space.
Solitude alone brings comfort,
Since it offers a pain-free embrace.
Aloneness... nothingness... darkness...
These are my shades of solitude.
They cannot hurt me."

The words above were written years ago
By a scared little girl in pain,
Trapped in the grasping clutches
Of toxic turmoil and terror personified.

Young and powerless was she,
And although she tried to flee,
She was held captive in a home
With guarded, secretive insanity.

-2-

Decades have passed since that sad time,
But inner healing work
Has hurled me back in time
To the scene of the crime.

Standing face-to-face with the little girl within,
I need to give her a great big hug
And soothe her pain, by trying to explain:

She was a helpless victim who was hurt,
and her beauty wasn't marred
because of someone else's dirt.

The lonely, frightened girl who wrote this poem
was abused, hurt, felt unloved, and all alone.
She needs to know she's worthy to be loved.

Her solitude protected her.
Her writing helped her to cope.
She has the strength to survive.
So she could emerge and thrive
Like the beautiful Phoenix
That is being reborn...

Now, as she dusts off the ashes,
She can see the precious vibrant gem
That was patiently sleeping beneath,
But was always there!

-3-

There were people in my past
Who have burned me with their fire of anger,
And slashed me with their scalpels of hatred...
Do the scars ever heal?

So the frightened little girl of times gone by
Only recently learned how to cry.
She's learned that numbing out the pain
Will only cause it to remain.

She thought if she could just be a rock,
The hardness would keep the pain away.
And if she could be an island all alone,
Sorrow and hurt would fall astray.
  She was wrong...

-4-

And now, perhaps, still a child to some degree,
I wonder if the truth will really set me free.
Since delusions and denial just prolonged distress.
False armor and guarded aloneness,
Didn't make the agony any less.

So, with stumbling fear,
As a child takes her first steps.
Then falls, gets scared, but then just tries again.
I will try to heal my wounds and then move on.

I will try to lock eyes
with the beauty which lies,
In the little girl within...

And finally release her
From the darkness,
And the shades of solitude.

Chapter 2 – Mothers

Old Photos

Sometimes, by piecing together
A visual biography,
A hazy hypothesis emerges
And becomes crystal clear.
Suddenly apparent,
Shockingly transparent.

Looking at photos
Of my mother's life,
I saw transitions...
From a smiling teenager,
To an adult woman
Who had lost her reason to smile.

And,
Since she could no longer smile,
She didn't want anyone else to smile either,

And she made it her life's mission
To make sure that this didn't happen.

The Serrated Steak Knife

It was a silver, sparkling
Serrated steak knife.
Used for cutting meats –
Not threatening someone's life...

And then –
One day –
That changed...

It suddenly became a weapon,
Pressed against my throat,
By someone
Who was supposed to
Love and protect me...

I will always remember
That steak knife...
The sharp, cold metal point,
And how it made me feel.
Scared
Shocked
Unloved
Hated!!!

As my mother held it there...

Time seemed to stand still
As she dared me
To utter
A
Single
Word...

The Toxic Dance

Year after year,
My mother and I
Engaged in
The debilitating
Dance of Dysfunction...

Bickering,
Escalation,
Explosion,
Estrangement,
Endless, Tiring
Pseudo-reconciliations...

Still, nothing actually changed.
Nothing was ever resolved.
We just kept on dancing
In the ballroom of toxicity.

Despite all of this, I couldn't permanently
walk away from this toxic relationship...

Because... well...
Because she was my mother,
Or, at least,
The only mother I ever knew...

There is no other explanation.

The Night My Mother Died

The sound of the phone ringing
Shattered the frozen silence of the night.
As the silence broke into little pieces,
I felt my heart begin to pound.

I knew what was coming...

It was 3:30am.

I hung up the phone,
And burst into tears,
Telling my husband:
"My... mother... just... died."

Then a dam broke.
Tears morphed into sobs.

Forty-three years of memories
Unmercifully assaulted me
All – At – Once.
I felt sad... angry... confused... guilty.

I felt cheated out of the closure
I wanted and needed to heal my soul.

I never thought how I would feel
On the day that she died.
As crazy as it sounds,
I never thought she *would* die.
Our battles had become
A part of my identity.
Now, I felt as if a huge part of me –
Also died along with her.

The Wake

Eerie silence permeated the viewing room,
Amplifying the thoughts in my head,
Forcing me to focus within.

My thoughts were a
Rapidly changing kaleidoscope
Of sadness and confusion,

Bouncing off each other
Like a turbocharged
Rubber spaldeen ball.

In eerie contrast,
My mother looked peaceful
For the the first time ever.

Suddenly, I wondered:
Did her restless spirit
Leave her body?

I thought about our relationship...
We had very little in common,
Well... except for the fact that

We were always disappointed in one another.
She couldn't live up to my expectations.
I couldn't live up to hers.

Yet, I just knew that
The huge influence she had over me
Would transcend her death.

I felt that
She was at peace,
But I would never be...

The Voice

It hit me like a lightning bolt!
I would never hear
My Mother's voice again...

The voice that
Annoyed me,
Argued with me,
Antagonized me,
Always criticized me.

The voice that kept silent,
Rather than offering kind words,
A compliment,
Compassion, or
Approval.

The voice that always sounded
Upset,
Angry,
Frustrated.

The voice that never ever said:
"I love you."

It's strange...
There were so many times
I preferred my mother's silence,
Rather than her disapproval.

And now...
She was silenced forever.

And the strangest thing of all is,
Sometimes, I still miss
Hearing her voice...

Tumbling Down

One moment, we were exchanging a gift,
The next moment, she shoved me off a cliff,
With No Forewarning.

(Or maybe, I just didn't want
To see the signs.)

While deeply immersed in hell,
Hope was devoured.
Chewed up and spit out
Into little lingering pieces.

Pit black darkness
Surrounded me.
No exits or end in sight

In the dark abyss of oblivion...

The aftermath of reading

My mother's words in her Will.

As my world
    Came
        Tumbling
            Down...

One Hundred Pennies (The Will)

"I leave my daughter, Nella Coiro, the sum of one dollar."

Which is: 100 pennies...
One – hundred – pennies...

Why?
Because I accidentally learned I was adopted?
Because I wasn't her biological daughter?
Because I confronted her about the incest?
Because I didn't enable her?

Her words in her Will morphed into
A hot blazing spear plunged into at my heart,
Ripping into each layer on my flesh

The intense pain brought me to a dark place,
Immersed sadness for a long time...

Decades later, I sometimes think about the 100 pennies
She sadistically threw at me,
As she escaped through death,
Like a spineless coward,
In the darkness of the night.

It took much inner work and reflection
To heal, and realize that
This was a statement about her,
And who she was.
And had nothing to do with me,
Or who I am...

She left quite a legacy...
And that's completely on her...

Chapter 3 – Adopted

Adopted

Handing me the baptismal certificate,
She said: "I see that you were adopted."
The clerk assumed I already knew.
But actually, I had no clue!

Beneath the facade,
I portrayed a coolness,
Even though I was
Completely clueless.

As this decades long lie
Rapidly melted,
By the blazing heat
Of a thousand suns,

My legs began to feel weak.
As my world began to crumble,
The ground seemed to
Tremble beneath me.

All – at – once,
I realized that, for 39 years,
Everything I thought
I knew about myself was a lie!

Emotions flooded my mind:
I was shocked and confused.
I was enraged!
I felt betrayed.

It was the most shocking,
Sad, surreal,
Heart shattering
Moment in my life.

The Screaming Truth

Betrayal and lies
Were disguised with a smile,
And gaslighting words
I've believed for a while.

But then, in a flash,
After decades have passed,
True colors bled through
And reversed what
I thought to be true.

Facts weren't forever concealed.
Eventually they dwindled, and revealed

The Truth,
Which kept SCREAMING to be heard!

It's was only a matter of time...

Origins

It feels strange and sad,
Sometimes even heartbreaking,
That I've never met my biological parents.

I've never heard their voices,
Or the joy in their laughter,
Or have felt their touch.

I often contemplate
Whom I might have resembled.
Who's personality I might have emulated,

Or, what my life would have been like
If I wasn't excluded from their lives,
And forced to be *the other*,
In my adopted family.

I contemplate my origins
Often.
Too often,
As if decades later
It still matters,

When it really doesn't.
Or shouldn't.

Does it?

Should it?

Dear Birth Mom

Dear birth mom:

I can't help but wonder about you –
The mother that I never knew.

I have always felt a void throughout my life –
A vague sense of infinite emptiness –
A missing piece of a puzzle.
Now – at least – I understand why.
There has always been
A gaping hole in my heart
That represented the absence of
Motherly love and caring.

I have a fantasy that we will
Meet and greet other,
When I enter the heavenly realm
In the afterlife.

We'll immediately recognize each other.
We'll smile, hug, and say *hi* to each other.
Then we'll have a cup of coffee together.
I don't know what we will say.
Does it really matter?

The point is this…
We will finally connect
And maybe, just maybe,

That lifelong gaping hole in my heart
That lacked the motherly love
Will finally be filled…

Chapter 4 – Sisters

a Free And New Non-toxIc lifE

Our toxic bond
Was flimsy and frail,
Shabby and savage,
Foredoomed to fail.

Her noxious games.
And covert schemes
Frazzled the relationship
Along the seams.

Boundaries were crossed.
Trust was breached.
Reconciliation is
Now beyond reach.

I've exited the cyclone
While I still had the chance,
And stopped engaging in
A venomous dance.

I've opened my eyes.
Released noxious ties.
Renouncing the strife.
Reclaiming my life!

I am now celebrating a
Free And New Non-toxIc lifE without you!

The Ice Queen
(Fannieng Toxicity)

The Ice Queen moves
like a thief in the night,
Insidious and Covert...
Assembling her flying monkeys
To dish out her dirt...

*Fannie*ng the flames of toxicity
And making sparks a bonfire.
With sadistic glee and insanity.
She dances on her celebratory pyre.

Gaining pity with skillful ease,
And gathering her allies
To attack her enemies,
Trying to cause their demise.

The Ice Queen is self absorbed.
Immersed in *me, me, me*.
There is no world outside of her.
She lacks human empathy.

The ice queen moves
Like a bobcat in the night,
Seeking out her prey.
Sending her surrogates attack
Whomever gets in her way...

Earnestly Earned Karma

I want to be the gruesome monster
Cast in the starring role
In all of your nightmares

Terrifying you
Every Single Night,
When you close your eyes.

Then you can feel the horror
You have fervently inflicted upon me.
Enjoy your
Earnestly
Earned
Karma…

Guitars & Lipstick

We were different teenagers,
My sister and I.
I focused upon music.
Her interest was guys.

She didn't care about strumming a tune.
She was focused upon makeup and perfume.
I didn't want to be dolled-up or tanned.
My dream was someday to play in a band.

She was a social butterfly.
I was reserved, quiet, shy.
She emulated my mother,
While I was seen as *the other*.

She picked up the lipstick.
I picked up the guitar.
We were complete opposites.
We still are…

The Competition

I will never forget my sister's words:
You know, just because you're on dialysis,
Doesn't mean I don't have
medical problems too."

Her voice had no empathy,
Or even a speck of sympathy.
Just her covert casual cruelty.
Self-absorbed in *me me me*,

I had just began dialysis,
It was a very troubling time.
A frightening, upsetting,
Arduous uphill climb.

While my sister never met an illness
She didn't fall madly in love with,
Or believed that she had.
While perfecting the ability
To gain desired sympathy.

She coldly appeared
Jealous and pissed
Because she could not
Compete with this…

I intruded upon her domain
Cultivated for years,
While perfecting
On-demand tears.

And then, within weeks,
The pent-up storm
Began to form,

And all hell broke loose...

Unreciprocated Love

It seems impossible
To love someone
Who consistently uses you,
And mentally abuses you.

Who lies and plays games.
Embraces trauma.
Continually creates
Unnecessary drama.

Someone who behaves as if
Regardless of how much you give,
It's not appreciated,
Often deprecated,
And simply never enough.

And yet, despite
Being used and abused,
There was a time when
I still loved my sister.

I don't understand why...

My Sister's Her-i-cane

I have gradually begun
To move toward healing,
And beyond feeling deeply

Saddened, Angry,
Hurt, Heartbroken ,
Devastated, Disappointed,

Since my sister deliberately
Dragged me through
A horrific hurricane,

Assisted by her flying monkeys,
Smiling and gloating,
As she left me there to die.

Now, in hindsight,
I recognize that
She was a traveling hurricane,

Bringing the storm with her,
And creating destruction
Wherever she went.

Since I was within her
Sphere of influence,
Unknowingly,

I was in Dire Danger...

Her Mother's Daughter

Sister coped by emulating,
Winning favor from our mother,
While I was dubbed the rebel,
And I became *the other*.

She is still her mother's daughter
In oh so many ways.
Replicating and creating
An ongoing toxic maze.

And so...
The legacy
Of dysfunction
Continues...

The Turbulent Winds

The debris and dust have finally settled...

Tattered and torn traces
Of destruction will linger –
As a reminder...

And the turbulent winds
Still carry the aroma
Of where they had been,

Permeating and disrupting
The tranquility
Of the present moment.

Sadness continues to linger
In tiny little bitesized
Pieces and breezes,

Sometimes they still
Revisit me,
Unwelcome
And Uninvited ...

The essence of the turbulent winds
With scattered scents of resentment,
Sadness, disappointment,

Are tattooed upon my heart,
And will remain forever,
Never to be forgotten...

Getting Wet

Should have stepped away sooner
From encounters inflamed.
Should have stopped making excuses
About dysfunction unexplained.

Instead...

I stood in her rain cloud
Without an umbrella,
And just pretended
The sun was shining.

Now, I've learned an important truth:
You can't walk through
Someone's thunderstorm,
Without getting wet.

Exiting Hell

It could have been so different,
the way you've treated me.
You could have shown some kindness,
and been a sister to me.

Your deliberate actions
Like a knife, pierced my heart,
And although you've hurt me deeply,
I chose not to fall apart.

And there could come a day
When you might feel dismay.
Perhaps with hindsight clarity,
You might see life differently.

When you're alone and pensive,
Perhaps some day you'll see
That you've wasted precious years
On a futile blaming spree.

I am moving past the sadness,
From your covert, vicious attacks,
I refuse to be your victim.
I'm so tired of your traps.

Now, on the wings of freedom,
I will swiftly fly away,
As I finally release your toxic grip,
I'll feel the warmth of the sun,
and a bright new day.

I will bid you adieu
without a single tear.
And as I walk away from hell,
I will leave you in the comfort
of your self-imposed despair...

Banished

Sister,
You have been edited and
Permanently deleted
Out of my story,

Along with the pain
That you have
Flagrantly, viciously
Inflicted upon me.

Sadly...
You've shown me that
I need to protect myself
FROM YOU.

I hope the karma you've earned
Will knock on your door
And visit you every day
For the rest of your life.

You have now been placed
Permanently in exile.
Banished to
The other side of
Never
Again...

Fading to Invisible

You've gathered allies with bayonets,
adding accelerants to the pyre –
Memories were burned to ashes,
from the devastating fire.

Moments and years,
and the history we've shared.
Facing the painful truth
that you have never cared...

Now, the boxing ring is empty,
and I exit, worn and tattered,
Stronger, wiser, and still standing.
Surviving the impact of a crash landing.

The games are over,
And no one wins.
Sadly struggling to release
the could-have-beens.

Forsaking fantasies
Of who I wanted you to be.
Realizing I refused to see
The Truth — The Reality.

So, as we go our separate ways,
I think about the years and days...
Watching memories float away
And vanish as they make their way
Into the clouds... (Yet never completely gone.)

As the relationship DIES,
And, as you gradually fade to invisible,
With tears of both sadness and relief,
I will say Goodbye...

Chapter 5 – Scraps of Sadness

Scraps of Sadness

My heart was once a grand ocean
Of salty tears that endlessly flowed.
I still remember that frightened little girl,
Who lived in a dark, blurry lifetime ago.

Vulnerable, sad, and helpless.
Feeling like a delicate flower
Trapped within a rampant tornado.
Struggling every waking hour.

At times, I would wonder:
Is the weather dark and dreary today?
Or... Is that just a reflection
Of the pulsating pain in my heart?

I was just a lost soul,
Trying to survive another day,
When twenty four hours
Felt like infinity...

And every moment was
An icy cold, dreary,
Endless January day.

Were there ever any sunny days?
If so, I don't remember them...

Or, were the tears and fears
Obscuring my ability to see them.

Carousels

Exiting from the dysfunctional din,
Weeping for what could-have-been.
Propelled into turbulence once again.
When will eating anguish end?!

Again, I'll go my lonely way,
Struggling to face another day.
Weary from the uphill climb,
Inhaling agony in double-time.

Grief and loss, regrets and tears,
Can weigh heavily upon the years.
The carousels that used to shimmer,
Now weary, tired, and so much dimmer...

Frozen in Time

It's perplexing how emotional pain
Transcends the passage of days and years,
While paralyzing rusty tears.
Instead, it is solidly frozen in between
The moments and seconds of time.

Pain doesn't have clocks.
It doesn't comprehend
The ticks and the tocks.

Instead, it lives and breathes
Within its own
Unique, undefined,
Ageless dimension.

Timelessly.

Defiantly Dwelling
Within the realm
Of infinity.

Bursts of Darkness

Depression sneakily hides among
Dismal, dingy storm clouds,
Enhanced with steroids saturated –
As hope and joy are abated.

At times, hovering inches
Above my head,
From the moment I awake
Until the time I go to bed.

Without my consent,
Sinisterly Stalking me.
An unwelcome companion
Who won't let me be.

Depression sneers and creates misery.
Shooting bullets laced with agony.
It has a Personality – A Pulse –
A Pounding heartbeat...

Depression has a memory.
It relentlessly
And unmercifully

Replays recordings
Of the most painful
Parts of my life...

And therefore,
It's an ongoing fight,
With strength and might,
To crawl toward the light,

And away from
The Bursts
Of Darkness...

Lost in Sadness

I've never died from emotional pain,
Or drowned in my tears.
Although, at the time,
These were my fears.

Yet, when I felt
Lost in sadness,
And grasped by
The clutches of sorrow,

Although sinister
Circles of darkness
Surrounded me,
And swirled around me,

With spirals of
Darkness...
Emptiness...
Hopelessness...

Even when engulfed
in a dark, frightening,
Smothering
blanket of despair,

For some unknown reason,
I did not succumb or die.
I absolutely refused to!

Instead...
Determined to rise above it,
I continue to bounce back
And survive.

Grief is a Sentient Being

Grief is about...
The debilitating pain of feeling powerless.
We have lost someone or something
That we value –
That we love –
That we need –

Perhaps someone or something
We feel we can't live without.
They're gone forever,
And we can't do
A damned thing about it!

The feelings of hopelessness,
Hopelessness, emptiness,
Sorrow and heartbreak
Are so palpable,
We can almost
See them,
Smell them,
Taste them,
Touch them
With our fingertips...

Grief is a sentient being.
It has a personality.
A heartbeat.
A life.
A soul.

You can sense and feel
It's oppressive energy,
As it wraps its powerful
Arms around you,
And refuses to let go...

The Colors of Sadness

The colors and shades of sadness
are putrid green and rusty brown.

Salty tears are kindling wood,
Igniting a blazing fire
Within my heart.
The land of Oz is so far away.
The yellow brick road is obscured.
And magic potions aren't real.

Lonely in a crowd,
Tasting – inhaling solitude...

The colors of sadness
Tightly grasp,
And hungrily
Devour me,
S-l-o-w-l-y,
One shade at a time...

Will the sun ever shine again?
Or, will my life just be
An endless, eternal, dark eclipse?

Sometimes I wish I could spray white paint
Over each one of my painful memories,
So I never have to see, feel,
Or agonize about them ever again.

Chapter 6 – Pensive Ponderings

Diamonds

I recall laboriously lugging
The cumbersome weight
Of pain and fear
Up a steep mountain,
In the dreary darkness
Of the night,
With no end in sight.

But then...
I remembered:
Adversity creates pressure.
Pressure creates diamonds...

It's been difficult to imagine
That someday
I could... I would...
Become a brilliant diamond...

But I'm gradually feeling
A gentle transformation,
So it's only a matter of time.

Letting Go

Sometimes we grasp & cling
To frustration, sadness, anger,
Resentments & disappointment,
Like a flotation device.

We're afraid to let go,
Terrified that we might drown.
And yet... Actually...
The opposite is true.

We hold on for dear life
To the very things
That actually prevent us from
Fully living our lives.

We spin around and around
On a merry-go-round,
Nauseous and dizzy.
Thoughts in a tizzy.

Yet we still stubbornly
Refuse to let go – to grow.
To just move on.
To simply carry on.

As our emotions freeze,
Like winter icicles on barren trees,
We tightly grasp and squeeze
Until our hands bleed.

We dismiss and ignore
What we actually need,
Still caught up in the past
Or a fictitious fantasy
Of what we think should be.

Less Lost

As I reflect, I realize that
Life has often passed me by
At the Speed of Sound,

In tiny little tidbits,
While I blinked my eyes,
Weary with Worry.

But...

When I finally began
To understand and accept that
I really *don't* know the future,
Or where my path is leading,

And worrying about the unknown
Is simply futile, and
Emotionally brutal,

I grasped onto acceptance,
And...
Just for a brief second,
I felt less lost.

Lucky Alex

I envy my hound, Alex.
He closes his eyes,
And within seconds,
He's sound asleep.
Not a single peep.
(I wonder what he dreams about.)

Alex finds incredible joy
Dwelling in the moment.
I'm pretty sure he doesn't worry,
Or ruminate about a thing,
Or what tomorrow might bring.

Like a shark, he only moves forward.
He doesn't embrace resentments.
He simply forgives and moves on.

I'm striving to be
More like Alex.

Touching an Emotion

I've often wondered
How it would feel
To touch an emotion
With each of our senses.

To touch,
To see,
To taste,
To smell.

To transcend,
To ascend,
And peer beyond
The spoken word.

To touch an emotion
With our fingertips.
To inhale the scent
Of its aroma.

To taste its texture and flavor.
To see its shape, size and colors.
To sense and feel its energy.
To meet its personality.

With would this experience be?

The Clock

As I rewind
The tape of memories,
Reflecting upon
Many years ago,
And many tears ago,

I recall living my younger years
Wading through the darkness.
Nearly drowning, yet stubbornly
Swimming against the tide.

Desperately trying to heal
Hemorrhaging wounds,
While paddling through
The memories and throwbacks...
The debilitating flashbacks...

In what felt like eons,
The years moved on and on.
And as I struggled to let go,
The tears flowed on and on...

The clock didn't hold its breath,
And wait for me to heal...
To catch up... to wake up...
To wo-man up...

But that was another time.
Memories, dreams,
And flashbacks.
Are an arduous uphill climb.

But it's never too late
To begin anew,
As I work toward bidding
The painful past "adieu"

Dreams and Lint

When I go to sleep,
My dreams are a synopsis.
Of struggles, fears,
Exitless dilemmas...

Saturated with
Adversity...
Danger...
Turmoil...
Being Lost...
Feeling Abandoned...

Yesteryears,
Childhood trauma
And PTSD
Cling to me,
Like stubborn pieces of lint,
When I close my eyes,
And drift into the world of sleep.

Dingy Memories

I want to let go
But my heart shouts "No!"
Disappointment – Sadness – Anger,

They stubbornly linger,
Like ominous clouds
On a stormy gray
Icy winter day,
Obstinately refusing
To disperse and go away.

Traumatic memories,
Dingy with grime,
Refuse to leave.
They transcend time.

Their pulsating pain,
Their throbbing energy,
Float through the years,
Causing heartbreak and tears.

The clouds still remain,
Spurting raindrops of pain.
My heart insists upon reliving
The sadness, disappointment,
And pain of yesterday.

I blame myself for not letting go.
What can I tell my heart
To convince it to leave behind
My traumatic past,
And release this burden?

How can I convince it
To move into the peace
Of the present moment?

Loose Ends

Loose ends of days gone by,
Fade into the sky,
Fervently waving goodbye.
By the clouds obscured.
Yet...
Is their return
Covertly assured?

Loose ends...
They linger and they hover,
Sneakingly hiding for cover.
But not gone for very long.
Easily triggered by a song.

Loose ends...
Put up a fight before they die...

Loose ends...
Do they really say goodbye?

The Stylus

I try to move on
And not look back.
It was a painful downhill climb.

But it's not easy.
I cling to the compulsion of
Going back in time.

Then why am I
So obsessed with this,
When it gnaws at my soul?

And why can't I
Simply let it go?
What the logical end goal?

I'm the stylus
On a record
That's stuck in a groove.

Struggling
To jump ahead,
But unable to move.

How can I just
Skip ahead
And not look back?

Move on to
The next song,
Not the former track…

Chapter 7 – The Dialysis Journey

A Bucket of Ice Water

"Nella, you need to be on dialysis."

These words hit me like
A bucket of ice water,
Leaving me drenched
With fear and anger.

Suddenly, the solid ground
Morphed into quicksand beneath me,
Along with everything
I thought – hoped– my life would be.

Faced with this frightening path,
I asked myself:
"Is it better to live or to die?
Fight or give up?"

The answer emerged,
Like clouds slowly moving,
Allowing the sun to reappear.
And there it was!

Surrender is not in my DNA.
I am a fighter. I am a survivor.
Surrender – is – not – an – option.
The words "I give up" aren't in my dictionary.

Weary or not. Tired or not.
Angry or not. Terrified or not...
My choice would be to fight.
I've never walked away from a fight,
And this was no different.

The Dialysis Path

Dialysis has been a tiring, perilous path.
Sometimes I feel like Don Quixote,
Silver sword in hand,
Bravely and frustratingly
Fighting endless windmills,
Yet never really winning a battle.

Sometimes I feel like
I'm trapped on a carousel
With no off switch,
Rotating in endless circles,
Yet never moving forward.

I'm waiting... waiting... waiting...
For the elusive phone call
That will remove me
From this emotional hell –
A kidney transplant...
Will it ever happen? I don't know.
And there's the problem – the circle of uncertainty.

What have I experienced in four years? Hmm...

The feeling of being painfully thirsty
To the point of physical discomfort,
Yet too afraid to drink
Because of strict fluid restrictions.
Going to sleep early
To escape this horrible feeling.

Or,
Struggling to take a deep breath
After a dialysis treatment.
Gasping as I walk up a few stairs.

Or,
The fear and anxiety of having a transplant.
Yet, at the same time,
Desperately wanting it,
Because I can't stand to live this way
One... Moment... Longer.

Or,
The anger, frustration, and sadness I feel,
And the tears that sometimes flow,
Because my body has cruelly betrayed me!
Or,
Feeling exhausted
Every... Single... Moment...
Of my damned life!
Or,
The overwhelming sorrow I feel
That I'm losing three days of my life
Every single week.
Because, on dialysis days,
I struggle to live my life
In any meaningful way.

I feel like I'm constantly
Holdings onto a flagpole,
Perpetually terrified, as I watch
Another storm approach,
And lightning bolts rip through the sky,

Hanging on for dear life, and
Waiting – hoping – for the storm to pass,
And move away from me,
Toward the ocean,
Allowing the sun to shine again...
But it doesn't...

At least... not yet...

The Dialysis Machine

Beeeep! — Beeeep!

Beeeep! — Beeeep!

The deafening, screeching sound
Of the tall, white, blinking,
Sinister dialysis machine
Shouting!

Arrogantly attacking my senses.
Slicing through the comfort of
My soft, warm blanket of serenity...

I can only sigh in frustration,
Although I really want to yell:
"God damn it! Stop that sound!
I'm trying to forget that I'm here!"

Eventually it ends,
Until...
Another machine
Repeats the same
Intrusive assault...

Dialysis, a Day at a Time

It's been impossible to have kidney failure
And not contemplate my own mortality –
The possibility I might die a lot sooner
Than I might have preferred. Ouch!

Dialysis is a physically and emotionally rough journey.
I feel like I'm on a battlefield – without a weapon.
A fully-armed enemy is hiding in a foxhole,
And I can't defend myself, or end the threat.

Its hard to shake off the sorrow that I feel.
Sometimes I cry because I feel so powerless.
Other times, I'm angry and frustrated
That my body has unmercifully betrayed me.

Sometimes the fear and the sadness grip me,
They unmercifully wrap their arms around me,
and they refuse to let go without a struggle.
Still... regardless of how I might feel,

I still go to my dialysis appointments.
Sometimes it feels like a part-time job,
Other times, a prison sentence,
depending upon my mood on that day.

Nonetheless, I try not to define myself
Solely as a dialysis patient.
I try to see myself as a survivor, not a victim.
I try to share my experiences to help others.

I must keep reminding myself
That I will not surrender
Without putting up a fight.
I refuse to let kidney disease win this battle!

Dialysis Reflections, Tongue-in-Cheek

How does one find serenity
In the dialysis center?

Re-focusing thoughts
Is a pretty good start.
Sitting in a chair,
Six feet apart.

Two hours have passed,
one hour to go.
I'm freezing my butt off,
Like I'm sitting in snow.

The dialysis machine,
So fierce and yet meek
Is helping me get through
Another rough week.

So, let's just pretend
we're all at the beach.
Though frankly, that's quite
One hell of a reach!

My butt's getting tired
From sitting in the chair.
Dialysis is helping,
But my butt doesn't care.

Now, forty-five minutes
are left on the clocks.

But I'm still freaking cold,
Wish I wore heavier socks.

I can't wait to go home.
I'm as hungry as hell.
Just thirty-five minutes,
And the machine rings the bell.

Chapter 8 – Spirituality

God's Presence

I can feel God's presence...
The spark of God within me...
With the same intensity
that I can feel my own heartbeat.

I experience God in different ways...
Gentle guidance, comfort, and hope.

In the physical world – in the beauty of nature:
I feel God in every rainbow,
Every blossoming tree,
Every flower that blooms,
A gentle summer breeze,

Every beautiful,
graceful butterfly
That catches my eye.

In the evening,
I've seen God's signature
In the vibrant, breathtaking hues
Of a magnificent sunset.

Every animal companion in my life
Has also given me a glimpse of God
Through their capacity
For unconditional love...

In the worst of times
I've experienced comfort
Feeling wrapped in a blanket of
God's love and protection.

Spiritual Simplicity

I'm a spiritual woman,
Or, at least,
I try to be...

When my eyes are focused upon
The God of my understanding,
I feel Herculean strength.
I'm able to ride the tidal waves,
And weather the worst of storms.

When I lose my focus,
And look away
For even a second,
I can feel myself drowning.

It's that simple.

Miracles

A miracle is simply
A shift in perspective.

When our perspective changes,
Our world – our circumstances
Look completely different...

That's the miracle!
This shift in perspective
Allowed me to see
That which was previously
Invisible to me.

Within this miracle,
I've opened my eyes, and saw
Infinite new possibilities!
Imagine walking into a dimly lit room.
There are many things we can't see,
but they're still there.

Then, suddenly,
A bright light emerges
To illuminate the darkness,

And we're shocked
To see everything that,
Just a second ago, was invisible.

New insights fill the room!
When our perception is shifted,
This changes things,
Including our choices and our future.
And... well...
That's huge!

Been There

I know what it feels like
To be frozen by fear,
Or to feel so alone,
Even among other people,
Including loved ones.

I know what it feels like
To imagine the future,
And see Only
Pitch Black Darkness.

On the other hand...
I believe that God loves me,
God is with me, and gives me
Courage, resilience, hope and strength.

Sometimes,
God has answered my prayers
By calming the storm,
So I could take a restful breath.

Other times,
God allowed the storm to continue,
Giving me the endurance
To withstand the storm,
So I could gather
Strength and wisdom.

God didn't take me this far,
Through so many battles,
To ever abandon me.
God will forever be
Just a heartbeat away...

Finding God in the Darkness

There were times
I was assaulted
By adversity.

Bombarded
By boulders, and
Belligerent obstacles,

Terrified...

Submerged within
The darkness of the unknown.
I feared I would fall
Into a bottomless pit.
The dark abyss of oblivion...

Yet, somehow,
I just knew...
I just felt...
I would *not* topple off a cliff,
And, if I did,
A power greater than myself (God),
Would catch me before I fell.

Since I'm still standing,
Apparently *Someone* did.

The Shroud
(A Simple Prayer)

Dear God,
Please gently lift
The darkness of the shroud,
And let me catch a glimpse
Of the sun behind the cloud.

Please push the darkness
far beyond my sight.
And pull the sunshine forward,
So I can feel
The warmth of its light.

A Silent Whisper

Serenity is safely snuggled
Beneath the clutter of thoughts,
That are often overwhelming
With shoulds and coulds and oughts.

Within this sphere of silence,
I have captured and embraced
Amplified composure,
with gentle, delicate grace.

Stillness, sweet and warm,
Within the eye of the storm,
Illusive and appealing,
Insightful and revealing.

And as I listen closely
I hear... I feel...
God's voice...
in
a
soft
silent
whisper...

Chapter 9 – Random Reflections

Peter Pan

He was Peter Pan in so many ways,
Held captive in a toxic, hazy maze.
Forced to forever remain a man-child.
His soul was sad, and he rarely smiled.

He tightly clutched
His alcohol and pills,
Escaping from a world
with frightening, rocky hills.

He continued clinging
to his props and stash,
As his hope was discarded
With tomorrow's trash.

While those around him,
Afraid, just closed their eyes.
And their perceived indifference
Just added to his demise.

He lingered for a while,
But then decided
It was too painful living
In a mind divided.

And so...
As hopelessness
Consumed and
Overwhelmed him,

He checked out...

(In memory of a loved one, who sadly died from a drug overdose.)

Forgiveness Revisited

Is everything forgivable?
I once thought so.
Now... well...
I'm not so sure.

Forgiveness isn't black & white.
Rather, it's more of a palette
With cluttered clusters
Of shades and colors.

Perhaps it's like the ocean tides,
Forging forward,
Ebbing and retreating,
Then inching forward again.

Nonetheless,
I'm left with these questions:

Do we forgive on different levels,
Or in increments?

How many times
Should we forgive someone
Who repeats offenses,
Or is unapologetic?

Are some things simply unforgivable?

How do we let go, and
Maintain the state of *letting go*
Permanently?
Is it humanly possible?

I don't have the answers yet...

Melting Snowflakes

Some people have floated through my life
Like clouds sailing through the sky,
Gradually obscured by the sun,
Or rendered invisible
In the darkness of the night.

Some have grown along with me.
Others followed a different path,
Sometimes through circumstance.
While some have exited with
Immature, unnecessary wrath.

Some have gradually dwindled away,
Like snowflakes melting
In the warm morning sun.
Others morphed from
A friendship to a shun.

Some were there for a reason.
Others for a season.
But few have lingered
For a lifetime...

Goodbyes

Goodbyes are complicated.
And has had different meanings
During different times in my life.

A *goodbye* can be liberating and healing.
A *goodbye* can be frightening, painful and sad.
Sometimes, it's a combination of conflicting feelings.
Throughout my life,
Many journeys have ended
With *goodbyes*,
Sometimes by choice,
Or due to other circumstances.

But every *goodbye* included a life lesson.
Sometimes an opportunity
To recognize my inner strength.
Or to heal and move forward.
Or to feel sadness,
And learn to gradually let it go.

Eventually all the tears subside.
We can't cry forever.
At some point, although saddened,
We must get on with living our lives.

Windswept

So here I am again...
Powerless once more,
And frightened to the core.

The facts of life are bold,
Insensitive and cold.
They've clutched me by the throat,
Forcing me to kneel.
They don't care what I feel!

Do struggles ever end?
Alas, I'm windswept one again.
I feel windswept once again...

If wisdom's born of struggle,
Does it ever really show?
Do we see it as vibrant fireworks,
Or simply a soft glow?

As the darkness bows to light,
And the day banishes the night,
When will I finally understand,
Or capture the depth of insight?

Do insights transcend
Both time and space?
Do the puzzle pieces
Gradually fall into place?

If I reach higher planes,
With less losses and more gains.
When I finally find the answers,
Will I be the last to know?

Will I be the last to know ...

Just Tales

To escape pain and grief, how often have I
Re-arranged the pieces of what I've perceived,
To give me some comfort and fleeting relief?
Though rough days feel endless,
A lifetime is brief.

Crumbling remnants
Of worries and fearful foresight,
Neatly buried in sand,
In the frozen silence
Of the night...

But... in darkness,
Like stars,
Fears illuminate,
And become blazingly bright.

I'm relieved by the slumber
That takes me away.
Then I open my eyes
at the dawn of the day,
Trying to blink all
My troubles away...

And poof... in a stream
Of steamy hot air,
They're gone for the moment,
'Til they reappear.

Embraced by brief comforts
Of fictitious details.

Convincing my mind
That security prevails.
But my heart and my soul
Knows that these are just tales.

Dream-mares

The path toward survival
Is a delicate flower,
Vulnerable and helpless,
Caught in the cusp of a tornado.
Struggling every waking hour.

Memories of yesterday's traumas
Feel gone... until I close my eyes,
and then, sometimes they revisit me
In my dream-mares...

I cannot outrun my nightmares.
They catch up to me,
As I drift off to sleep.
And, at that moment,
They are in
Complete Control.

Uneven Exchanges

I have stopped giving away
My power,
Like candy treats
On Halloween...

Trick or treat...
But the trick
Was on me.

Those whom
We allow
To control us,
Ultimately —
Own us...

NEVER
Give your Power
Away.

Unsteadiness

"If only..."
"What if..."
"Poor me..."
"Why, why, why?"

Is standing on a cliff,

Wobbling...

getting ready

to lose

our balance...

Carousel of Absurdity

I used to worry
About
The opinions
Of others.

And then,
I realized that
They were actually
Thinking about
Themselves,
(And not me!)

And probably
Worrying about
What *I*
Thought about them…

This is
The carousel
Of absurdity…

The Sidewalk

I notice the foolishness...
Of tripping and stumbling
Into the same cracks
In the same street,
Again and
Again.

Until...
I've grown weary and tired
Of hobbling on crutches,
And
FINALLY
Learned the lesson...

Still,
I wonder why
It takes so long...

Gashes & Slashes

Do we ever truly heal
From the agony and torment
That others have
Caused us to feel?

Or – from
The gashes
And slashes
Of life?

Or – from losses
That have shattered our hearts
Into infinitesimal,
Shredded pieces?

Do our painful triggers
Gradually lose
Their sting?
Their Intensity?

Does the anguish
Attached to the memory
Fade
With
The
Passing
Of
Time?

I don't know...

The Measure of a Life

How do we measure
the value of our life?
Count the moments of wisdom,
or the hours of strife?

How much growth we've achieved?
How much love that we've shared?
Through the lives that we've touched?
Or the people who cared?

As the moments become days,
And the days become years,
Is our joy within our laughter,
or our wisdom in our tears?

Do we measure our growth,
by the paths that we traveled?
Are our insights the sum of
the truths we've unraveled?

Is there a way to perceive
how much worth we possess?
Did we cling to our worst,
Or put forth our best?

And when our lives approach
the setting of the sun,
Can we be proud of our achievements
And the things that we have done?

Battle Wounds

I turn my back to the ominous wind,
and weep for the should and could-have-beens.
Into turmoil I descend.
When will tasting anguish end?

And so, I'll go my lonely way,
Dreading each minute of the day.
So weary from the uphill climb,
inhaling stress in double time.

Nightmares of the hornet's nest...
Mourning all the moments missed.
Is life, then, just an futile quest
In search of reasons to exist?

It was Alcohol

It became deceptive courage,
And reckless bravery.
It was a pseudo-scholar.
A guru of con-artistry.

It was a fantasy lover,
Charming and romantic.
It was calmness – it was excitement.
Tranquilizing – Frantic.

It became a pseudo-parent,
Nurturing the emptiness.
It became a living hell,
Creating agony and distress.

It was a spiritual undertaker,
Laying the dead soul to rest.
It distorted human potential,
Enhancing worst – destroying best.

It was a slow consuming cancer,
A ruthless killer, with lies to tell.
It was a demon dressed as a prophet,
Promising heaven, dispersing hell.

It was dressed in lavish clothing,
Skull and crossbones concealing.
It was sensuous and alluring,
Seductive and appealing.

It will take you to the heights of ecstasy,

Then send you crashing down unmercifully –
Causing you to die in fragments...

Behind the optical illusion ...
And soul-crushing confusion...

It was alcohol...

A Patient Boomerang

Karma is a loan
From a loan shark
Yielding a high interest rate...

At a snail's pace,
Unexpectedly...
Eventually...
Inevitably...

The boomerang will
S-l-o-w-l-y
Make a U-turn...

It's only
A matter
Of time...

If you live long enough,
You might notice that
Life is...
A patient boomerang ...

Insomnia

Within the stillness and silence,
And pitch black darkness of the night,
Sleep has abandoned me.
Said "Good ridden."
Now stubbornly hidden.

Taunting me, mocking me,
As it grinned and frowned,
And now, poof in the air,
It is nowhere to be found.

Helpless and frustrated,
I lay there in bed,
As thoughts obsessively
Swirl through my head,

From one, to the other,
to the other,
to the other...
Increasing in speed...
An emotional stampede!

Memories – sights & sounds – replay
Like a vinyl record
That keeps on skipping...
With no end in sight.
Repeatedly...
Over...
And over...
and over...

The Curse of In-som-nia

The Middle

Life is a tally sheet
Complicated. Bittersweet.
Bumps in the road.
Shocks, roadblocks,
And surprises untold.

Have you ever felt frozen
Within space and time?
Bewildered by the absence
Of reason or rhyme?

Or trapped at the crossroads
Of forward bound?
Feeling far more
Lost than found?

A magnet pulling you
Back to the past,
And as hard as you try,
You can't seem to get passed?

Does enduring indecision
Obscure your vision,
As emotions create
Debilitating Division?

Captured in the clutches
Of in-between
Clinging to bunches
Of what-has-been.

The intersection of "The Middle."

Snapshots through Time

As my younger years
Spin through my mind
Like photos on a carousel,
The spinning slowly stops,
Allowing me to see
What is – what was – the total me...

Bits and pieces meshed together
Through the years, drenched with rusty tears.
Murky memories now seem a hazy dream.
Did yesterday really exist?

There were those in my childhood
Who have used a Sharp blade!
Deliberately thrusting it into my heart
with compulsive conviction,
Reminding me
That I would always be
The *unwanted other.*

Happiness and peace were
As fluid as the sand.
Slipping through my fingers
And my grasping hand,
So quickly, that the experience
Was rapidly lost.

Life lessons that I've learned so deeply
Have rendered me consumed with pain completely.
At that moment, feeling I would die,

But somehow I continued to survive.
But do I feel –
More or Less
Alive?

Chapter 10 – Growth, Healing & Enlightenment

The Meat Grinder

I recall the memories
Of a frightened, helpless little girl,
Who's spirit was maimed
Every single day.

Placed into a meat grinder
And ground into bloody
Little chunks and pieces,
S-l-o-w-l-y and P-a-i-n-f-u-l-l-y.
Inch-by-inch.

Sadly,
This shattered, scattered
Mangled, pulverized spirit
Followed her into adulthood...

And now,
With much healing work,
Her spirit is being
Reclaimed,
Rejuvenated,
Reintegrated,

And gradually,
Cohesively
HEALED
Inch by inch...

From gushing blood
To gushing hope!

The Darts and the Dart Board

We we all have a critical invoice,
A nasty little gremlin...
It whispers in our ear,
Points out our weaknesses,
Our negative qualities,
Our mistakes.
It frightens us,
Prevents us from feeling joy
From loving ourselves,
Or give ourselves credit
For our accomplishments.
Stops us from forgiving ourselves.

This critic is throwing darts,
And we are
THE DART BOARD!

Now, I've taken that dart board,
Collected the darts,
And set them both on fire!

Goodbye & good riddens
Inner critic.
I am control now!

Glinda's Words

When I was a forlorn child,
Unwanted, berated, reviled,
With minimal reason to smile,

I pleaded and prayed
For a swirling, whirling tornado
To embrace and whisk me away –

To Somewhere, Anywhere,
To a place – a world
Where I felt safe and loved.

I preferred Dorothy's wicked witch,
To my frightening mother.
Dorothy's witch was far less terrifying.
I've also identified with Dorothy,
Feeling helpless and afraid. Overwhelmed!
Trapped and lost in a frightening realm.

I too have followed a yellow brick road,
Pushing past the road blocks
That obscured my cluttered abode.
Like Dorothy, I've sought external solutions.
It never occurred to me to look within.
Not knowing – that's where solutions were hidden.

As a child, I pondered Glinda's words:
"You've always had the power, my dear.
You just had to find it for yourself."

And eventually, albeit decades later,
I finally got what Glinda's was saying,
And so... I did just that!

Bubbling Hot Coffee (Trauma Drama)

Everything was a potential tragedy
In my immediate toxic family...
"Laugh today, cry tomorrow.
Life is filled with nothing but sorrow."

Doomsday and Drama
Were always brewing,
Like a hot pot of coffee
Ready to bubble over
Unexpectedly... at any second.

My family's predetermined conclusions:
Trust no one. Everyone's out to get you.
Sneezing... you might have a pneumonia.
Too thin... you probably have cancer.

If it was drizzling or raining, uh-oh!
My family was ready to collect wood,
And, like Noah, build an ark.

In the past, I, too, had a tendency,
To fear, yet be allured by
That insidious hot pot of coffee.
Fearing, yet waiting for it
To bubble over!

Now, the coffee pot doesn't scare me anymore.
I have control over it. Not the other way around!
I worry much less. I try to live my best life

Calmly and gently, quietly and easily.

Gradually, I am becoming
The woman I want to be,
Without ominous bubbling coffee pots
And exhausting, endless trauma drama.

Recovery

The recovery journey is life changing.
Requiring determined dedication.
Including an emotional revelation,
A complete lifestyle excavation.

I've seen people bounce back
From the worst of circumstances.
Evolve from the depths of despair,
And through their share,
Teach others how to repair
Their own lives.

I've learned that faith and hope
Can soothe and heal all wounds,
One Day at a time, or sometimes,
An hour or a minute at a time.

The tenets of Recovery programs
Have helped me through
Every – Single – Difficulty
In my life.

Soul Mate Reflections

Who am I?

I see the best parts of myself,
when I see a reflection of me,
As I gaze into your
Nonjudgmental eyes...

One reason I love you
Is because you understand me
Better then
 I understand *Me*.

You see beyond
My blind spots...

Precious memories and reflections
Gently tossing in the wind
Upon the wings
Of a soft summer breeze...

My love for you
Transcends space and time.

(Dedicated to my husband Kenny)

Changes

"This too shall pass."
Is hard to manage
When captured in
The grips of challenge...

Yet, I try to peer beyond
Fear and frustration,
And see every event
Has a specific duration.

Life events continually
Change like the seasons.
Sometimes without
Warning, or logical reasons.

As the earth keeps on spinning.
And the seasons keep changing,
I've gathered some wisdom
That accompanies aging.

I've met seasons of darkness
And winter days, dreary.
Moving ever so slowly,
Making me weary.

Then as Spring emerges
And steps into my view,
It sprinkles tinted tidbits
Of nature now renewed.

"This too shall pass"
Always echoes and stays
As the seasons propel me
Through the changes in my days.

Dancing in the Rain

I used to gather wood
To build a sturdy ark,
To protect me from the rain
and the impending dark.

Preparing for the storm
That never happened.
Wasting energy
Of tragedy imagined.

But now I'm learning
At the pace of snails,
To discard the wood,
The hammer and the nails.

To live in and embrace
The moment that I'm in.
To step away from
The imagined din.

To enjoy the changing sky,
A sunrise – a brilliant golden hue.
Or the colors of a twilight:
Orange, purple, pink and blue.

I'm now finding joy
In a subtle, simple thing,
Like a crisp December day,
Or the emerald shades of Spring.

Or watching my dog
Dance around so excited,
Happily munching on his treat,
Tail wagging, delighted.

Or my hubby strumming
His electric guitar.
Singing a song,
As I sing along.

I've now disembarked
From the trauma-drama train,
And I'm learning to prance
And to dance in the rain...

Evolving & Becoming

Life didn't get easier
As the decades
Melted away...
I've gotten stronger,
So it just
Felt that way.
I am astonished,
Frustrated,
Exasperated,
That it has taken a lifetime...
Tiring,
Gut-wrenching
Decades...
To learn
Simple lessons...
How many sunrises
And sunsets
Have crossed my path,
To bring me to this
Enlightened
Moment
In
Time?

Animal Companions

My animals have been my greatest teachers.
I've learned about enjoying the present moment,
And being loved without conditions.
There's joy in seeing a happy,
Wagging tail just for me.
And an animal who loves me
And doesn't care about my flaws.

Each special relationship I've had
With each of my animals
Has helped me to grow,
And become a better person.
I can't even imagine
The emptiness I would feel,
 If I didn't have an animal in my life.
We need to love ourselves
As our animals do.
Completely..
Unconditionally
Boundlessly
Abundantly
With bursting joy,
And infinite gusto!
Now that's a helluva lot of love!

Purple Hearts

It's interesting how the bruises and scars
That I've endured in my life
Became a Personal Purple Heart.
A symbol of Honor and Bravery.

In hindsight, each roadblock in my life
has given me some valuable tools
To endure the next one.

It has taken a lifetime
Of healing my bruises,
Bouncing back, and
Gathering strength,

To see... to feel...
Understand, appreciate
My resilience,
My inner beauty,
My strength,
And gentle fierceness ...

My Inner Knight

My Thoughts and Memories
Of the horrors of my past,
Have been Powerful,
Invasive. Pervasive.

They've have trapped me
Behind a barbed wire fence
With a gate that's locked.
Entrance blocked.

Preventing me from
Moving forward, and leaving
Days that have passed,
In the past.

Remnants of residual fear...
From past memories
Their oppressive energy
Still lingering in the air...

They've prevented me
From exiting this maze.
The misty memories
Creating this blurry haze.

But then, my *inner knight* in
Glistening armor, weapon in hand,
Fearlessly forges forward...
And takes command.

Rescuing me from
The sleazy cesspool of the past,
The rusty memories
That still haunt me,
The blurry ghosts
That still taunt me.

My *inner knight* brings forth within me
Crumbs of resilience,
Morsels of strength,
Tidbits of hope,
As I s-l-o-w-l-y inch forward
Beyond all obstacles.

My brave *inner knight* rescues me
Helping me to battle & shake off
Ruminations, mental invasions,
Obsessive attention, stressful reflection,
Of yesteryears...

As I take a deep healing breath,
Exhale the past, and hug and cling to
The present moment,
One heartbeat at a time.

Paying Attention

In my younger years,
Overwhelmed by memories and tears,
I failed to live in the present moment.
I did not pay attention!

I missed moments of beauty:

Sunrises at dawn,
Welcoming the day.
The colors of a sunset,
Like a floral bouquet.

New leaves on the trees.
A gentle spring breeze.
Twinkling stars at night.
The splendid moonlight.

Thinking back, I wonder:
Where did the time go?
How did it pass by so quickly?

How many moments did I waste
Ruminating about yesterday?
Worrying about tomorrow?

How many beautiful
Sunrises and sunsets did I miss?

Now I work hard to focus
On the moment I'm in.
Where I'm going,
Not where I've been.

I try to enjoy each moment.
I am learning to pay attention!

Forward Bound

I'll turn my back to the wind,
and wave goodbye to the should-have-beens.
Walking away from yesterday,
and breathing the air of a fresh new day.

The years have swiftly flown away
while I was focused on yesterday.
The past has weighed me down too long.
Today I'll be choosing a new song.

I'll walk with my head held high,
As my eyes are forward bound.
The past is gone. I'll be moving on.
It's time to spread my wings and fly!

The sun has set on yesteryear.
I'm weary from shedding rusty tears.
I am seeing my life with fresh new eyes.
Choosing to bid the past goodbye.

Walking with my head held high,
my heart is forward bound.
The past is gone. It's time to move on
as I spread my wings and fly!

Sticks & Stones

When life threw sticks and stones at me,
I had two options:
Allow them to hurt and defeat me,
Or,
Collect them, and build a fortress.
Use them to my advantage,
To learn and to grow,

In my youth, I allowed them to crush me.
As I've matured, I've learned to choose the latter.

My personal growth
Has allowed me to see,
It was always a choice.

Still Standing

My life has been... well...
Often Overwhelming.

Yet, I'm still standing!
I'm not the woman I was
Decades ago.
Sometimes I think,
Who was that person, and where did she go?

I have evolved
From a scared, and often terrified little girl,
To a more empowered, courageous woman.
I'm happy about that.
Yet, I'm frustrated that it took so long.

I've learned to expect the unexpected,
To gradually accept the unacceptable,
And acknowledge that life is filled with
Loose ends and unanswered questions.

And although I don't remember
Every moment of my life,
I do remember the epic moments
That have changed my life.

Sometimes I feared I would drown, but I didn't.
Instead, I clung to the waves of each storm,
Afraid, yet with unyielding determination,
And I have survived. Albeit, not without scars.

But the point is this: I've survived!
And really, that's all that matters.

Moments Etched in Time

Regardless of the passage of time,
Some moments and words are never forgotten.
They have transcended years,
And live in the realm of timelessness.

Some have brought tears to my eyes,
And have torn me apart.
Others has replenished my soul,
And brought joy to my heart,

Some are as comforting
As a hug – gentle and warm.
Others are quite jolting,
Like an electrical storm.

Every smile and every tear
Has an indelible story to tell.

We can select
The moments
We choose
To focus upon.

The Phoenix

There were those
Who have charred me
with their flames of anger,
And slashed me
with their scalpels of hatred.

And yet…

I had the strength to survive.
I did emerge and thrive.

Through the work that was done,
The battle was won…

Upward growth
toward the rising sun…

Darned with golden sashes…
dusting off the ashes…
The Phoenix rises!

Intoxicating Toxicity

Toxic family healing
Has been a gut-wrenching,
Long, Laborious, Life Journey.

Sometimes, when I reflect back,
I think I've shed way too many tears
Over those unworthy of a single teardrop.
Yet, at the same time,
Each teardrop has rendered
Cleansing, purging relief.

Healing allowed me to exhale
Much of the toxicity
I inhaled and ingested
When I was around
These individuals
Who were intoxicated by
Their own toxicity.

Transfusion and Rebirth

Emotionally transfusing
The poisons of a toxic family
Has been an arduous endeavor.
It still requires ongoing effort.

It's been taxing to shed
Old layers of myself.
Becoming a new me,
Completely toxic free.
Yet, I've made great strides.

If the different versions of me
Were to meet each other,
they would meet as strangers.
They wouldn't recognize one another.
Maybe they wouldn't even like each other.

This process is like dying
And reincarnating as someone else
– a completely different person.

Long Story Short

Long story short...
You've enjoyed
Tearing my soul apart,
And shattering my heart,

At the same time,
You've enlightened me,
And helped me to find
Strength of mind.

Bouncing back stronger
And, now, no longer...
A puppy, lost and frightened.
Instead, my fierceness was heightened.

You've assisted me in growing,
Energetic resilience flowing
And seeping through my being...
Empowering and freeing.

Long story short...
You set me on fire.
But I walked thru the flames,
Dousing your games.
Emerging stronger

I am now Fireproof!

Long story short,
You couldn't eat me alive.
You helped me to thrive.

Long story short,
I survived...

My Life Manuscript

How I choose to live in this moment,
How I choose to live this day,
Will influence my tomorrow.
In a deeply significant way.

How do I want my story to end?
Who do I want to be?
Who do I want see
When I cross over this bridge,
And permanently dwell
On the other side of adversity?

I must remind myself:
I am completely in control
Of how I want
My life manuscript to read.

We all are...

What Is Hope?

Hope is the belief that although we feel like our life is crumbling, and we are going to fall off a cliff, something will catch us and keep us from falling.

Hope is about ignoring all of the evidence that, right now, things seem dismal and will not get better. It is the ability to look beyond that. To look beyond the clouds and see the sun peering through, if just for a moment. Or, at least, even if we can't see the sun right now, to know that it's there and will eventually appear.

Hope is mustering up the courage to forge forward, even thought we might feel weary, or angry, or terrified. Even though we feel that we don't have an ounce of energy left.

Hope is not denial. It isn't putting our heads in the sand, and hiding from how difficult the road ahead can be.

Hope is facing all of the roadblocks that might stand in our way, and choosing to seek solutions, despite the frustration or fear that we might feel.

Hope is absolutely refusing to give up without a fight.

Amid adversity and ongoing challenges, I've always had hope, even if it was just a smidgeon.

Sometimes hope was the only thing that kept me going, as I daydreamed about better days to come.

What if?

What if…
We stopped looking at our differences
And, instead, focused upon our similarities?

What if…
We worked on our own shortcomings,
Before judging or criticizing anyone else?

What if…
We looked beyond race, ethnicity,
Lifestyles, or religious beliefs,
And recognize that we all share similar pain,
Struggles, fears, hopes or dreams?

What if…
We were open to hear other points of view,
Even when we vehemently disagreed?

What if…
We no longer felt a need
To defend our position?

Namaste means the spark of divinity in me
Recognizes and honors the spark of divinity in you.

What if…
We recognized, respected and honored
The spark of divinity in each person,
Rather than focusing upon
The clashing of our egos?

What if....
We could work toward spreading
The spirit of *namaste*
Around the globe, one person at a time?

What would our world look like then?

Epilogue

T.S. Elliot beautifully described life journeys: *"We shall not cease from exploration, and the end of all our exploring, will be to arrive where we started, and know the place for the first time."* As my work on this book of poetry comes to an end, I can definitely identify with this quote.

As with my memoir, *Dancing in the Rain*, at times, it was also difficult, painful, and overwhelming to share my experiences and feelings in this book. It has also been cathartic, healing and enlightening.

In my life, I have learned that every challenge, obstacle, and trauma has helped me to gain strength, resilience, and courage. Despite all of the roadblocks that I've encountered, I've learned valuable lessons, gained wisdom, and achieved personal growth and healing. I've learned that sometimes complete closure isn't possible, and accepting this with grace can often offer some sense of serenity and peace of mind. I've also learned that it helps to have acceptance, flexibility, and, sometimes, even a sense of humor.

Most importantly, although sometimes I still have difficult moments, especially since I am currently on dialysis, which is emotionally and physically challenging, I still identify myself as a survivor, and despite some limitations, I can still find joy in my life. It also helps to keep reminding myself that my current situation is not my final destination.

This *survivor* label is a very healing perspective which continues to assist me in growing and bouncing back. It is my hope that if you're able to identify with any of my life experiences, you too will see that you can transcend your own challenges and roadblocks, and eventually recognize that you are a survivor too. I also hope that my poetry might help you to find your inner strength.

We all have our own personal snapshots through time. Further, I believe that I am, and we all are, ongoing encyclopedias of life lessons. These lessons only have value if they're shared to help someone else. This is what I am sharing my experiences with you.

A Message from the Author

I am grateful that you've taken the time to read *Snapshots through Time*. I hope you have found some level of comfort, inspiration, or healing from the heartfelt words in this book. I value and appreciate your feedback, even a brief sentence, so please take a moment to leave a rating and comment on Amazon, or another retailer or website where you've purchased this book. Thank you so much!

Other Titles by this Author:

- **Dancing in the Rain** - *A Memoir of Courage, Strength, and Resilience*
- **The Forgiveness Journey** - *Transcend Your Hurt, Transform Your Life*
- **The Forgiveness Journey Workbook**

Acknowledgements

To my husband, Kenny. Thank you for your, support, insights, encouragement, and for being such a loving life partner throughout the years.

In Loving Memory

Remembering my basset hounds: Penelope had a big, unforgettable personality. She has helped to teach, challenge me, and change me in significant ways, and has taught me to be a better person. Patrick, aka Mr. Paddyman was a sweet boy who was a gentle and lovable soul. He especially enjoyed being hugged and cuddled. He has taught me so much about loving without conditions. Run free, my sweet baby girl and Mr. Paddyman, my fur children, until we meet again in heaven.

www.ingramcontent.com/pod-product-compliance
Lightning Source LLC
LaVergne TN
LVHW011707060526
838200LV00051B/2799